AF230067

Sacred Flute

Sacred Flute

Poems

John C. Mannone

Iris Press
Oak Ridge, Tennessee

Copyright © 2024 by John C. Mannone

All rights reserved. No portion of this book may be reproduced in any form or by any means, including electronic storage and retrieval systems, without explicit, prior written permission of the publisher, except for brief passages excerpted for review and critical purposes.

Cover Photo:
Albumen photographic print of a Yuma musician
taken by I. W. Taber between 1870 and 1912

Book Design:
Robert B. Cumming, Jr.

Library of Congress Cataloging-in-Publication Data

Names: Mannone, John C., author.
Title: Sacred flute : poems / John C. Mannone.
Description: Oak Ridge, Tennessee : Iris Press, 2024. | Summary: "Sacred Flute by John C. Mannone is a book of poems infused with and inspired by Native American Indian culture, history and legend. This collection focuses on Native American nations on the North American continent"— Provided by publisher.
Identifiers: LCCN 2023052516 | ISBN 9781604542677 (paperback)
Subjects: LCGFT: Poetry.
Classification: LCC PS3613.A56825 S23 2024 | DDC 811/.6—dc23/ eng/20231109
LC record available at https://lccn.loc.gov/2023052516

Acknowledgments

I am thankful to the venues listed below for having published some of the works in this collection:

300 Days of Sun: "The Last Train"
The Acentos Review: "A Psalm of Flowers"
Anacua Literary Arts Journal: "Ayuhwasi," "Monarch"
A Tapestry of Voices, Knoxville Writers Guild Anthology: "Tanasi"
Aurora in the Sun, Aurora Wolf Press: "Song of the Sun"
Bosphorus Review of Books: "Transition"
Credo Espoir: "Morning Has Broken"
Curio Poetry: "The Lizard Wind"
DoveTales, An International Journal of the Arts (Spring 2015): "On a Quite Walkway"
The Dribble Drabble Review: "Medicine Man"
Frontage Road: "Border Patrol"
Hinchas de Poesia: "Guatemalan Fruit Fields"
Mildred Haun Review: "The Ant Hill People"
MO: Writings from the River: "Magic Water"
Mystic Nebula: "Mythic Stars"
North Dakota Quarterly: "The Night the Stars Fell"
Nthanda Review: "Pangaea"
New Fairy Tales, Aurora Wolf Press: "The Storyteller"
Red Coyote: "Little Wishing Star," winner of 2018 Tennessee Mountain Writers 'Writing for Young People Award,' "The Siyotanka," "Whisperings"
Sequoyah Cherokee River Journal: "After the Felling of Trees," "Staurolite"
Songs of Eretz Poetry Review: "Dreamcatchers" 2014 finalist; "A Voice of Waters," "Ceremony"
Tennessee Magazine: "The Trees Wave Their Branches," 2nd place winner May 2016
Triangulation: Habitat, Parsec Ink: "In Plain Sight"
Trickster Journal: "The Uncovering" ["el destape" in Spanish]
Tupelo Press 30/30 Project, March 2014: "A Self Portrait," "Dreamcatchers"
WINTER WRITES—*Poems, Stories & Sagas*, Whitesboro Writers, Jan 2016: "Surviving Winter"

To *Kwanita*, my beloved, which in Zuni means, *God is gracious.*
The Sioux speak of her as *winchinchala* (a girl to fall in love with)
who says to me, *Koshkalaka—I am yours altogether.*

Introduction

Sacred Flute is a collection of poems infused with and inspired by Native American Indian culture, history and legend, and are not necessarily redactions—these poems are transcendent of that.

This collection focuses on Native American nations on the North American continent.

An association to a particular Native American nation is made whenever possible. In many cases, the poems were directly influenced by those traditions of the represented Native American nations, but in other cases when it was less clear, the sentiment was recognized as American Indian and an appropriate connection was sought and found. Each major section is also introduced by the such. At times, the connection is made through an epigraph or in the body of the poem, at other times, it is through a postscript.

Bibliographic and Internet sources that have influenced and/or informed these poems are cross-referenced with bracketed numbers in the body of work.

Attempts have been made to at least capture the major Native American nations, either directly or through their language groups.

Contents

I.

Land & Nature

Song of the Stars

We are the stars who sing,
we sing with our light;
We are the birds of fire,
we fly over the sky.
Our light is a voice.
We make a road for the spirits,
for the spirits to pass over.
Among us are three hunters
who chase a bear.
There never was a time
when they were not hunting.
We look down on the mountains.
This is the song of the stars.

—Abenaki-Passamaquoddy song [1]

Mythic Stars

We stood alone at the precipice,
its edge cutting the near darkness,
moon glinting hints of silver

on tarnished leaves of the empty forest
below. And the stars glimmered.
We watched them night after night

until they disappeared behind the light-
washed skies, caravanning across
the desert space—sand, asphalt black.

Shiny clusters here and there: phantasms
of all the wild creatures we imagined.
And they could see us, too. One night,

the black oozed like wet tar in the heat
of the night. The stars dripped
their glossy oils and glittered earth.

The hot stars danced into the night
entwining each other as if threads
spooling filaments of light. Knitting

tissue, sinew to bone. Warping skin
over framed hearts. They fashioned
themselves. And when they were done,

looked back to the empty heavens, then
pawed, hoofed, slithered and crawled
to place their shimmers of magic back

to constellation the ancient sky.
It was pleasing. My wife asked me,
What will you call them, Adam?

See Note [2]

The Trees Wave Their Branches

*O Great Spirit, help me to always speak the truth
quietly, to listen with an open heart and to remember
the peace that may be found in silence.*
—Cherokee prayer [3]

The sway of the poplar tree
—its canopy thrust into
the quiet rush of wind—
its quake of leaves, I hear that
hush, too, the brush against
sky. I read their chlorophylls
and auxins, their lean into light.
Arms stretched, beckon for
the company of birds to nest,
to give them rest from predators
and storms, and listen to their cries,
their songs breaking the silence
cradling the dawn.

After the Felling of Trees

I still hear the mountains
cry.

The woodsman swung his mallet,
drove the agile wedge midway
into the rail of oak. Split pieces
hung in air, as if in disbelief,
before they lumbered to the ground.

They lay offset, bark to dirt,
hearts splayed open.

Many leaves
shed.

Postscript: *When all the trees have been cut down, when all the animals have been hunted, when all the waters are polluted, when all the air is unsafe to breathe, only then will you discover you cannot eat money.*
—Cree Prophecy [4]

A Voice of Waters

The river speaks
a language of crisscross patterns
spills secrets of the sun
hidden in ripples whose glints
spangle the bright blue air

the river smiles like the universe
or what we think are endless smiles
but space and time are not infinite
only indifferent and full of darkness
yet blackness is not infinite either

the river speaks
as its undercurrents slowly
rise to the surface
washing over rocks
by the banks of the evergreens

Postscript: *"The water speaks the same way: God says, feed the Indians upon the Earth. The grass says the same thing: feed the horses and cattle. The earth and the water and the grass says, God has given our names and we are told those names. Neither the Indians or the whites have a right to change those names. The earth says, God has placed me here to produce all that grows upon me... the same way the earth says it was from her man was made. God on placing them on the earth... said, you Indians who take of the earth and do each other no harm. God said, you Indians who take care of a certain porton of the country should not trade it off unless you get a fair price."*
—Chief Lawyer [5]

Pangaea

Walk lightly in the spring; Mother Earth is pregnant.
—Kiowa [6]

The land unraveled at the seams
when the flexing began, red core
pushing from deep down inside.
Mother Earth convulsed in labor
giving birth. She bled blue rivers
to oceans capped white in wind.

I think of you, but my heart
ruptures in the same way hers did
two hundred million years ago.
Sutured now, mountains stitching
earth; rumpled skin, healed.

Or was she? We cast her aside,
I see only rubbled slopes, trees
fallen, not even an acorn left.
We breathe insolent green air
in her face, her green eyes fading.
In a blink, she will be gone. Far

away, wedging the horizon
—flamingo red, heron blue—
black and white cranes,
wings shearing the folds of sky
before they're gone... as you.

II.

Identity

My face is a mask I order to say nothing
About the fragile feelings hiding in my soul.

—Glenn Lazore (Mohawk) [7]

Magic Water

Lead gray Sawtooths jut above horizon
cut into Idaho sky spilling its blue
over frozen lava flows.

I stood looking at the water, still as crystal.
She bathed the baby in the cool tranquil lake,

wrapped his caramel skin in finest fleece—
inked mosaic of eagles dancing
to sacred music of the earth.

I heard soft echoes of his cries
pry loose Shoshone secrets from the ancient rocks.
She hushed him with lullabies—

shaman hymns, in rhythm of her arms,
washing sleep over his eyes,
clear and onyx black.

Tanasi

Eventually, all things merge into one, and a river runs through it.
The river was cut by the world's great flood and runs over rocks
from the basement of time. On some of the rocks are timeless raindrops.
Under the rocks are the words, and some of the words are theirs.
I am haunted by waters.

—Norman McClean [8]

The Cherokee had a way with words.
Before their nation became the State
of Tennessee, they called it Tanasi,
the place where the river bends,
where the green water meets itself.
From the foothills of the Smoky Mountains,
the Cherokee, the Creek and the Yuchi
could see the confluence of rivers—
the Holston and the French Broad
that gave birth to the Tennessee—
And so could the German, French and Irish,
and the English, too.
Each in their own language spilled words
as blood, which would wash through
the ages into the Tennessee. Today,
I hear their whispers in the dogwoods,
their honeysuckle prayers, the swish of voices:
Sequoyah, Boudinot, John Ross.
When I breathe their names, I hear echoes
of generations hovering over waters,
their swollen fingers reaching out
over the great expanse of the valley.
These people who fashioned this land,
their tears still flow into the Tennessee.
Some have evaporated to heaven, yet fallen
again refreshing the land, but some left a trail
of tears. I am silent. I sit on the bank and listen
to my own heartbeat measure that silence,
to the flow of the river over rocks, to the sound
of words there. To the sound of many waters,
the voices of nations.

A Self Portrait

On the back of a Native American painting
in the Koshare Indian Museum, La Junta, CO

I saw myself
I saw myself singing
I saw myself living
I saw myself happy

—Taos after Kause

What is there to fear? The thundering
hooves of a White Buffalo? The White
Spirit spoke to me in a dream, whispered
that I was fashioned in his likeness, with
even softer words, *Look into the still lake*
I see you through your eyes, and when
the eagle flies through the water-sky, know
that I am looking through its eyes, too.
Do not be afraid of your own image
for you are looking at me. Your soul is safe.
…I will let the artist paint my image.

My smile rippled the water, shimmered
oak trees and their leaves, as if a wind had
breathed a song through their falling tears.

The Storyteller

The old man, skin like butternut shells,
body twisted as a hickory stick, hunches
over the Chippewa campfire. His eyes burn

with reflection, glassy as a night owl's,
could count the feathers of a nighthawk
flying in moonlight.

His ears large and fluted, tuned
to whispers of an underground mole
whose breaths whooshed as thunder.

When the rivers and lakes are frozen
and the snow has drifted deep,

hunters and their wives, with children, wait
for the Storyteller to begin. They believe
everything he says as they listen to his tales

of bears with fire eyes and dragon claws,
of butterflies with wings large enough
to fashion sails for birch canoes, and
of green serpents with golden manes of horses.

He said, once he found a water lily, its leaf
so broad, it made a dress for his wife.
And a bush that grew so large as he walked,
it took him all day to hobble around it.

One summer evening, he shot an arrow
without taking aim, pierced a swan
and twenty brace of ducks swimming
on the river. It flew through the hearts

of two deer on the bank, bounced back
off a limestone rock, and as it skimmed
the water, killed the king of salmons before
it could spawn. He remembers

when the oldest red oak was just an acorn.
He said, he will be alive long after our enemies
have disappeared from the land of our fathers.

Tomorrow, the Storyteller will visit
the Cherokee, or the Navajo,
our brothers, whom we do not know.

See Note [9]

Tennessee State Symbols

Walking Horse (originally bred from Narragansett and Canadian Pacers crossed with Spanish Mustangs), Bluetick coonhound, Raccoon, Mockingbird (with more than 200 calls), Bobwhite Quail, Eastern Box Turtle (yellow-splotched carapace to mimic the winter leaf of tulipwood), Smallmouth Bass, Channel Cat, and the Appalachian *Plethodontidae*—the Tennessee Cave Salamander (about to lose its home).

Honeybee (*Apis mellifera*, its sweet product, honey, not as valuable as its pollination—one-third of all our food; endangered by 'colony collapse disorder'), Firefly (enchanting the summer night with a dance of luciferin lights), Ladybug, Zebra Swallowtail (upon which some can whisper wishes).

Iris (orchid-lavender and floral emblem), Tennessee Cornflower (petals bursting like a purple crown of sun, and wild), Passion Flower, Tulip Poplar, Eastern Red Cedar (indigenous evergreen, a red juniper with a sacred scent). Tomato (a nightshade, like American Beauty, a very old, nearly forgotten heirloom from Peru).

Agate (a cryptocrystalline quartz), Tennessee River Pearls (from mussels in Caney Fork shoals, swift and shallow), limestone (often rich in fossils), Pterotrigonia (a Cretaceous bivalve in the lime-rich muds of clay and silt and relics of the Coon Creek Formation).

Davy Crockett, Dolly Parton, Morgan Freeman, Aretha Franklin, Minnie Pearl, Dinah Shore, James Agee. But where are the Cherokee?

Wiȟópeča Okínihaŋ[1]

After the *Dignity of Earth & Sky* Sculpture by Dale Lamphere

She casts a peaceful gaze across the waters of the Missouri River. During the day, the South Dakota wind brushes the diamonds in her star quilt, causing blue shades to twinkle in the sunlight. At night, she stands illuminated and strong. She is Dignity. [travelsouthdakota.com]

She began as a dream

in the South Dakota plains
and shape-shifted into a stature
of stainless steel strength and kindness.

Determination burnishes in her eyes;
her stance, sure against the elements.
She is a poem wind-breathing beneath

the crossbeams. She is resurrection,
beauty spilling her sacred mettle.
                    Soul-fabric.

Father Sky and Mother Earth embrace
their daughter—she is one with them
and with her sisters. She is the beautiful

face of many Sioux:
Black Shawl, Her Eagle Robe,
One Who Walks With the Stars...

She is *Wash'aka*—strong, powerful.

She is fierce-gentle mother who fights
for her children, she has many arrows
of peace. She is warrior-queen—red cloud

in her eyes, pretty owl, yellow moon crying.
She has knelt with wounded knee, heart broken
by hatred. I cry with her, a cry for battle,

a cry of anguish, a cry for children,

and for her brave men.
     A cry for dignity.

Her breath carries voices
from the past, whispers of the future.
She is *a symbol of respect and promise.*

She outstretches a star quilt woven
metallic, and blue, and diamond-shaped
fluttering in prairie wind.

But she tight-holds, her fingers
curling inward toward her heart
pulsing with the blood of nations

       High honor
   Humble beginnings
New dawn

In morning's glory she glitters in the sun.
She glows peace at night. She walks on the edge
of land and sky, sacred river below,

with Lakota prayers on her lips. In the magic
of the wind, distant drums and rattles echo
through history, tambourine the air. She inspires

her descendants—we are mere tumbleweed
and dust at her feet, yet we offer
promises to keep the land sacred, it is

the heart of everything that is, promises
mix with sage-smoke—*Peji Hota*—rising
past her tender-strong hands, wisp up

to neck and shoulders, spiral
   to her smile of approval,
      and to the Thunderbird above.

---

[1] a stuningly beautiful, honorable woman

III.

Love

Hold on to what is good,
Even if it's a handful of earth.

Hold on to what you believe,
Even if it's a tree that stands by itself.

Hold on to what you must do,
Even if it's a long way from here.

Hold on to your life,
Even if it's easier to let go.

Hold on to my hand,
Even if someday I'll be gone away from you.

—Pueblo Prayer [4]

The Uncovering

The full moon rises. And crows caw,
their eyes sore from bright snow
blanketing hills. Uncovered mountains
chance a kiss on purple twilight. And I
desire a lovely Chippewa maiden.

I will toss her a plum-stone and see,
then tempt her with sugary, red plums
growing in the green field by the lake
that catch the crimson from the sky.

Veiled in shadows that spider across
its skin, the sacred moon—a dark red plum
peeled by edge of night—slowly
reveals its heart bleeding with light.
My heart uncovers. And crows caw.

See Note [10]

el destape

Llena, la luna se eleva. Y los cuervos graznan,
sus ojos doloridos por la nieve brillante
que cubre las colinas. Las montañas destapadas
arriesgan un beso en el crepúsculo púrpura. Y yo
deseo una hermosa doncella Chippewan.

Le tiraré una piedra colorada y veré
después seducirla con dulce ciruelas, rojas
creciendo en el campo verde cerca del lago
que captura el cielo carmesí.

Velada en las sombras que se mueven como arañas
sobre su piel, la luna sagrada—una ciruela roja oscura
pelada por el filo de la noche—despacio
revela su corazón sangrando luz.
Mi corazón se destapa. Y los cuervos graznan.

Spanish translation by the author

On a Quiet Walkway

Off Laurel Mountain Road
Great Smoky Mountains

We stepped into a place without clocks.
Where the shadows of leaves and light
Pendulum'd across our faces in the breeze.
By a stream, rhododendron on the banks
Drank laughter. Time gurgled, washing
Over each boulder. I kissed you there
For the first time. Our hearts tossed
With the same laughter, metronomed
Tomorrow. Today only leaves quiver
Keeping time.

Postscript:

Don't walk behind me;
I may not lead.
Don't walk in front of me;
I may not follow.
Walk beside me that we may be as one.
—Ute [6]

Little Wishing Star

An adaption of the Chippewa legend
"The Story of the Star and Water Lilies"

The world blossmed young and without winter,
and gazing down to Earth, a bright little star
wished to live there among the children. It grew

lacy wings, hovered close to trees, but wept when
it lighted inside the white rose high on the mountain.
It was lonely there. So it floated down to the prairie

to live on blades of grass, but soon feared the huff
and hooves of buffaloes. So it lay on a moss-nestled bluff,
but sobbed the children could not climb so high.

So it prayed and prayed by the glow of the moon;
it wished and wished by the twinkling stars' tunes
and soon would learn just what it should do. In a flash

it's face lit up. It swept down to the surface of the lake,
where the frogs would sing and the fish would simply look.
The children could safely row in their sleek canoes

to see the spark-like flickers in the bright white lilies
shimmering all the lake. Water ripples would ease
into their tiny hands cupped to gathered up the soft

white blossoms, where inside the heart of each,
the little star would dwell, always in their reach.
And the children laughed, and laughed, and sang.

See Note [11]

Dreamcatcher

asabikeshiinh, Ojibwe word for spider

Like the shape of circle across the sky that the sun
and moon travel, its hoop is fashioned from willow
filled with webbing, the nettle fibers stranding rim.

Before the sun rises to burn nightmares in the dawn,
an *asibikaashi,* a spider woman, weaves a magical
web to sift the restless thoughts while we all dream.

Will she weave one for nations since the world is asleep
to crimes against humanity? I weep. Can we not be as
little children who are only frightened by the sandman,

the unknown darkness, or monsters lurking under the bed

of their imagination? Is this not a better fear to conquer
than the grown-up fears of humankind, which are real
monsters that eat our freedom, but sadly are dismissed?

And *I* need the *Asibikaashi* to slip the soft, calm thoughts
through the hole in the center of the web, to glide down
the hawk feathers, that wisdom dwelling in the quiet night.

I need good dreams to intoxicate my heart with images
of you and magic of the moon glistening on the silvery web
moving ever so gently in the window, in the tender breeze.

The Siyotanka

*The Siyotanka is a flute only for love music
to a winchinchala—a girl to fall in love with.*
—The Legend of the Flute of the Brule Sioux

Many generations ago, my people
played drums, gourd rattles, and bull-
roarers, but no flutes.

Night came deep inside a thick woods
with no moon, full of haunting hoots
and the groaning of trees in the wind.

Then a new sound: mournful, ghostly-sad,
but beautiful. A young hunter mostly had
a dream of a redheaded bird,

its woodpecker rhythms lulling him
to follow it as it flitted through the thin
trees. It lighted on a cedar, hammering

the branch like a fast-beaten drum,
and through those holes, a wind
whistled like a flute.

He took the hollowed piece of wood
back to his village and stood
in a holy place to purify himself

while crying for a vision in his dream.
The branch he whittled, so it seemed,
into the shape of a long-necked bird

with beak wide-open. He painted one end
the sacred color red, then rubbed on
the incense of cedar, sage and sweet grass.

He fingered the wood-pecked holes, softly
blowing into the mouthpiece. A song, ghostly
and beautiful drifted all the way

to the girl he's been so long desiring.
She heard the moaning, the crying
sound of the siyotanka while in her's father tipi,

lying on her robe made of buffalo,
by the fire. She was compelled to go
outside when she heard the music

of the flute. She saw the young man
standing under moonlight. She knew then
it was her lover. She said, *Koshkalaka,*

I am yours altogether. So they lay down
under one blanket and she became
the hunter's wife, and he, a great chief.

Beautiful love-music hung on all the leaves
as it traveled through the air and cedar trees
from tribe to tribe.

———————

See Note [12]

IV.

Dark History

*There can never be peace between nations until
it is first known that true peace is within the souls of men.*

—Oglala Sioux [6]

Border Patrol

Men watched
wave after wave
approach their border
crude weapons
slung over shoulders

        They wandered their land
        Wondered if it could stand
        the influx of disease

The men crouched
hid their faces
cracked as clay
baked red in the sun

        They wandered their land
        Wondered if it could stand
        the violence of invasion
        the inversion of their world

Through the bush
they stared
wave after wave
washing in

        They wandered their land
        Wondered *Is this not our land*
        our children's?

The men feared
kept watching
wave after wave
They could not stop them
even with prayers

        and they came

      La Pinta
          La Niña
             y La Santa Maria

See Note [13]

The Medicine Man

After "The Dawn Sprinkler" by Virgil Nez

My face hides behind a mask
    wearing smiles of the gods

In my blue hand, a gourd rattles beads from a cactus plant
    whose needles have fallen unto dry ground

I squeeze a handful of feathers and mourn
    the eagle to find peace in the shadows of the wind

The skin on my skin has turned to the color of hope
    and I sing to the goddess who sparkles the twilight sky

I pray to her to change the dream—the blue-green
    of my desert land to what it once was—warm amber
      sifting through my fingers before they came

The Guatemalan Fruit Fields are Beautiful in the Sun's Glow of Planetary Risings

When Jupiter burned the night, and Venus blazed the morning, when they hung together in twilight like fire gems in shadow of the sun, they heralded war and sacrifice, while others picked strawberries glistening in the Mayan dawn.

Land & Sky

South Dakota graves
Yellow bird in winter cries
Black earth with gold dust

and blood

Big-foot elk bugle
Echoes heard in Montana
The Blackfoot runs deep

over scarlet stones

Bannock skies pierced blue
Sunlit land kneeling wounded
Sawtooth silhouette

Idaho red

Ayuhwasi

Cherokee word for large meadow

An ice wind blows
over the bones
of the Hiwassee River

and the ancient camps
—a staging area
before the great migration…

also for Sandhill cranes
—black snowflakes,
silhouettes,

hundreds of them,
thousands, wings
raised in prayer

as they fly over the trail
of tears; they shed
feathers. And respect

falls from heaven
like an ever gentle
wisp of mercy.

At the Tennessee Sandhill Crane Festival, January 20, 2019:
Hiwassee Wildlife Refuge and site of the Cherokee
Indian Removal Memorial and Museum. Birchwood, TN

V.

Apocalyptic

Don't be afraid to cry. It will free your mind of sorrowful thoughts.

—Hopi [6]

The Lizard Wind

Tobacco was given to us
by the one who made us.
After a Blackfoot legend

The lazy man planted
no tobacco. In secret,
he took the medicine
man's. Others prayed
no mercy for the thief
—only for the lizard
to appear quickly to him
in dreams.

~~~

There is a smell
of rain in the air:
leathery & moist.
The desert slithers
under torn clouds,
the prickly cactus
full of blood red
juice. It's not safe
to lurk in the dark,
even though monsters
are only full of sand,
their windy shadows
are full of teeth.

See Note [14]
~~~

Surviving Winter

Campfire logs spray incandescent ash:
fireflies that once brushed against stars
pinned to the mountain sky. They fall
slow as dust to earth. To Earth, they fell
as meteors—just comet dust & debris
the size of mountains. I no longer see
the stars, and the Appalachians are all
covered with gray ash. Winter is long
and I am hungry, only a pot of soup
from a few dried berries gathered
last fall simmers. My wife and baby
lay under thick blankets, they're dead
asleep in the patched but tattered tent.
Soon, we will collect porpupine quills
to finish the blanket. Our dog is gone.

Things were a little different before.
The sky was blue and the fire licked
the bone chill off the very long nights.

See Note [12]

The Night the Stars Fell

November 13, 1833
Wichita Mountains, Oklahoma

And they were awakened by the light of falling stars.
And they ran out into the false day and were terrified.
They thought the world was coming to an end.
                                        —N. Scott Momaday [15]

Some two or three hours after midnight, small shooting stars began to be
observed in the sky which gradually increased in number and magnitude
until the whole firmament appeared in motion with them, as if the planets
and constellations were falling from their places.
                                        —The New York Evening Post

When the stars began to fall before the snow
moon, the Kiowa blood in my veins grew cold

and my heart began to winter. I prayed
to the rock spirit to hold my mountain together.

I prayed to the sky to take the chill
of death away, bearskins could not warm me

as I watched my sisters tumble down from skies
and my warrior brothers fall free from heaven,
        their souls shining

bright, sky blazing with their spirits, fire-tears
mixed with sadness as my people were emptied
        from their sacred place.

What kind of spirit would cast them out?
I knew it was a bad omen. The sky cried twice:

After the geese had gone, and the wolves howled
all night—the stars left a long trail,
        tears streaking the eyes of spirit sky.

The Leonid meteor shower that night were exceptional with over forty
per sec or 150,000 per hour blazing the skies. An equally frightening
Quadrantid meteor shower also occurred on January 5, 1834. [Indian
Removal Act, 1830; Trail of Tears, 1838]

Staurolite

Inspired by the Cherokee legend of fairy stones

Sleep comes harder these days
and digging in the Georgia red clay
doesn't help depite the ache,
even in my muscles. But I drift off
with a staurolite stone in my hand.
How curious
this mineral I unearthed, a cruciform
crystal, red-brown, like the warm color
of my skin. My mother told me about
these stones, how my happy ancestors
were dancing inside the magic of spring
around a crystal clear lake. They were
fairies
playing with naiads & wood nymphs
until the sun was covered in black
with a sackcloth weaved in darkness
of sin, and the lake had turned scarlet
from the blood
of the moon. Birds
stopped singing. An elf stepped out
of a broken tree, whispered sadness
of what he witnessed two thousand
years ago.
After they heard
what was done to the Promised One
—the holy man who could undo evil
unleashed by the Trickster after
Father Sky threw him down—
they wept heavy
tears on the trail, anguish crystallized
in all the fallen drops, shaping into
beautiful crosses
like the one I found—it has powers
to bring future promise. I squeezed it
so hard I awakened from slumber
praying

for my pain to dissipate, for my love,
my wife to return to me
                    from the other side.
When I gripped the stone, blood trickled
from my palm, but it wasn't mine.

Author's Note: (a) From seven miles below the bosom of the Appalachian mountains, high temperature and pressure caused the penetration twinning of staurolite, an iron aluminum silicate called fairy stones or fairy crosses. (b) The poetic structure also shows a twinning of poems. The embedded one could be read: *How curious / fairies of the moon, birds / After they heard, they wept heavy beautiful crosses / Praying from the other side.*

In Plain Sight

For a moment, I put down the book on Kiwigapawa literature to my lap, rocking chair on my porch moves to the slow rhythm of words still drumming in my head, and the waning sun purples the horizon. I wince at the careless litter flitting in the high plains breeze, plastic wrapping itself in the twigs of a cottonwood. Soon the prairie will disappear into the black, but sagebrush will be silvered with starlight.

I ponder the heavens: what I learned at Reservation school—the Hubble Space Telescope imaging the *Deep Field* of mythical night when it stared through a "keyhole" in the Big Dipper for eleven million seconds—and now I imagine galaxies clustering like beads of dew on tumbleweed of dark matter, each with their own countless lakes of fire—all the stars bowing, singing in celestial amphitheaters. A hymn to creator *Kechi Manito*.

When I zoom in on those fiery jewels, see worlds orbiting them, some strange and cold with cryogenic volcanoes made of organo-plastics, while others team with a multiplicity of life so diverse and gorgeous like ours, it coaxes tears. I imagine if that intelligence were to peer through their keyhole and see our world orbiting a yellow sun arcing around a black hole in the center of our galaxy, our Milky Way, would they think any less of us? Would they deduce we worship a stage full of plastic milk bottles clustering around its own kind of darkness? Or would they see the magnificent beauty that still prevails?

Kiwigapawa refer to themselves as Kickapoo

Ant Hill People

Inspired by a Hopi legend

Once the world was destroyed
by fire. Stones from the sky burned
the air, convulsed the mountains

which vomited lava, oceans boiled.
Then destroyed again by ice
when the poles shifted. Floods, too.

Now there is a pestilence
that I see breaking loose
on the news, I wonder

of the consequence. Do we pray
as before, "Save us or let the rocks
fall on us?" Make it quick.

But to whom do we pray?
To the angry one with fire
in his eyes?

Great grandmother spoke
of passage into a new world—
a new heaven, a new earth.

But I sit and wait for a sign,
a cloud of hope, a pillar of light
leading me to the Ant Hill people.

They will take me to the caves,
teach me how to survive
on beans, or grow a beanstalk

to heaven if I am good enough.
Great grandfather would say
none of us are

but believes the Great Spirit
loves us anyway. For a moment
his eyes were almond-shapes

as he raised his shiny, spindly arms
in praise; stood up proud and
danced, his head puffed-up as
big as the moon full of light.

See Note [16]

VI.

Spirituality & Healing

*If anyone desires a wish to come true they must
first capture a butterfly and whisper that wish to it.*

*Since a butterfly can make no sound, the butterfly can not reveal the
wish to anyone but the Great Spirit who hears and sees all.*

*In gratitude for giving the beautiful butterfly its freedom, the Great
Spirit always grants the wish.*

*So, according to legend, by making a wish and giving the butterfly
its freedom, the wish will be taken to the heavens and be granted.*

—American Indian Legend [17]

A Psalm of Flowers

After "El Vendedor de Alcatraces"
—Diego Rivera (1941)

I have put all the lilies of the valley
in my basket, carry them with me.
And you, who have made them all,
are buried in the petals, lost
in the color, in the silk white texture,
in the smell lingering
over them, over me, with fragrance
of prayers brushing your feet.

Whisperings

A butterfly flits with a broken wing
hinted ochre and copper brown.

Ever so slightly, its plaintive whispers
hover over white umbells of boxwood

blooms swaying next to honeysuckle
that clings to anything its vines can clasp.

Sweet floral esters incense the desperate air
as if rosary prayers wisping heavenward.

Deep in the fields, seal brown horses
stir. Rolled hay—altars—offer sacrifice

to the wind, wheat strewn among the dried
grass whisper hints of fall, of spring dying.

Hollow straws fragile as bones, break as I
walk on them, air rushing out as if final

breaths of *Ruach*—a whispering to Father
Spirit to dispatch his angels. Do you hear
                              their whispers?

Inspired by a legend of the Tohono O'odham Nation of the American
Southwest that the butterfly would carry wishes and prayers to the Great
Spirit, which is always granted in exchange for setting the butterfly free.
[18]

Mending

Before the buck and kick,
the whinny and snort,
       I see you gaze at me
in the shimmer of your eye.

Which one of us will break
first, give in to the other's
stallion will?

I feel the wet gleam
of your wide-eyed questions
in those mirrors
       and the brokenness

washed with ebb and flow
of your heart, my heart—
       so many ripples
in the sky-blue there.

No, you are free, I will yield
but not break
either you or me, yet I am
       on your bare back

holding on for dear life
to the silk of your mane.
       I hear horse whispers
in the wind.

Postscript: *Great Spirit sent the message in the wind… whenever an Indian needed help, they could hear the hoofs of the Wind Horse come to them in the blowing wind. His spirit would comfort them until the tribe could arrive.* [19]

On the Edge of a Nature Trail

Do you know that trees talk? ... I have learned a lot from trees: sometimes about the weather, sometimes about animals, sometimes about the Great Spirit.

—Walking Buffalo [20]

I ask a poplar tree
interrogate its leaves
      jostling in a swift hush—
      the language of trees
only the wind understands
until the sun louvers through
      and thoughts bend
      with the light.
Questions of the sky
answered
      in the mystery
      of a poem.

Walking Buffalo (1871-1967), also known as Tatanga Mani, was of the Nakoda nation in Western Canada.

Morning Has Broken

Through the gauzy valley light

Sifting through the windowpane
I see a solitary lily illumined

On the edge of a dark green field
Its petals cup the balm of daybreak

Clusters of vitreous and translucent
Pearls of dew in the pale red light

Of last night's dream

Postscript: The soul would have no rainbow if the eyes had no tears.
—Minquass Proverb [21]

Kokopelli

They call me a medicine man | because I have an MD from Johns Hopkins | yet my wife cannot become pregnant. I wish | Kokopelli would jump down from the full moon, hunched-over with the spirit | of music, divine feathers | protruding from his head as he plays his sacred flute of fertility (he can bring his lovely flutist, Paiyatamu)—perhaps there'll be a chord stricken, a resonance for my wife, and I.

He carries unborn children on his back | for Hopi women | so why not for us, too? | My mother prays | to St. Gerard Majella, patron saint of fertility and pregnancy | I do not pray for zealous sex. That's not the problem—I am not a desert fly either | with a prominent proboscis and rounded back | nor am I a trickster that my wife could never trust | yet, like Kokopelli, I feel emasculated.

Instead, I will pray to the God of Kokopelli for tender love and understanding | for healthy sperm and egg | for perfect temperature and timing | for right chemistry—pH and pheromones | and for no societal judgment, regardless of what happens | no cultural misappropriation | of the Divine.

See Note [22]

Dark Matter

Humankind has not woven the web of life. We are but one thread within it. Whatever we do to the web, we do to ourselves. All things are bound together. All things connect.

—Chief Seattle [23]

Tonight, the sky is full
of Milky Way stars

        I remember the Hubble
        staring through the keyhole

supposedly an empty place near
the handle of the Big Dipper

        for a million seconds,
        the Deep Field exploding

into several hundred billion
galaxies like ours. I ponder

        the questions of physics
        like Galileo and Einstein,

of myself, the mysterious
darkness that equations

        cannot answer. I fall asleep
        inside the vast cosmos

of my mind. And I dream
of my ancient people with

        whom I am one. I want
        to know who I am. I ask

my brother, but he asks
me first. The prairie wind

        blows dust into my face
        and hair, yet I lift my eyes

to the heavens,
the arc of stars

        brushing light at my feet.
        The dust of them,

the moans of the galaxy,
cries for me. In darkness

        threads of light unravel
        some of their secrets.

I understand the heavens
within the heavens

        clumping together with
        the same mystery

that connects us all.

VII.

Afterlife

We will be known forever by the tracks we leave.

—Dakota [6]

~~~

When it comes your time to die, be not like those whose hearts are filled with the fear of death, so that when their time comes, they weep and pray for a little more time to live their lives over again in a different way. Sing your death song and die like a hero going home.

—Shawnee, Chief Tecumseh [24]
~~~

Monarch

The chrysalis glitters like blown glass
hanging from a Christmas tree. Sun sifts it.

Transforms the fragile bulb to an orange-laced
black with enamel-white spots—patterned silk.

One hundred million unfold: a royal symmetry
of Monarchs that marathon toward the sacred

slopes of Sierra Madres two thousand miles away.
But many are netted and jabbed by spiders, snagged

in claws of cats or pincer'd by birds' beaks.
There is no forgiveness, there is no gentle rain

when it pelts them to the ground, wings folded
in prayer as they are flushed into gutters. I hear

their screams, the spirits of Popoluca Indians
crying for refuge this day, *dia de los muertos,*

seeking the deep green sanctuary. The forest
umbrellas the survivors on their warm trunks.

They cloister among the leaves of oyamel firs
to mourn; flower clusters at the foot of graves.

But in the spring, they resurrect, unfurl wings
to catch the spilt sun. Waves of butterflies bloom

into flight and wash north to the Great Lakes
fulfilling their legacy. In ritual, each generation

flitters closer to home, but dies, until the fourth,
born to carry the spirits of the dead once more.

See Note [25]

The Last Train

The Great Spirit rolled a magical ball
crushing mountains, earth and rocks,
blazing a trail to the land of the afterlife.
The Great Spirit led the Indian chief
where the rolling globe of fire took them
—to see where his wife had gone—
if he would promise to grieve no more.
—Ute Legend of Canyons [26]

The railroading sun firewheels
the metal-sharp horizon

scorching night's edge
purpled with Indian Paintbrush.

Cirrus clouds wisp as engine steam
from some imagined train stack

clinkering the turquoise sky blue-black.
And the orange blossom moon,

with the last car pulled in solitude,
clacks invisible tracks.

Gotta catch that train,
gotta catch that train.

I jump across the gulch,
hands latching caboose, feet dangling

in cool thin air above red-blazed dust
stirred-up. The desert sky

full of sagebrush clouds, and below,
the river roars through the trestled gorge.

Gotta catch that train,
gotta catch that train,

whooshing through.

Song of the Sun

Do you hear her, feel the whisper,
a hush of wind warming the cold
corner where you are?

She'll shed her veil, let you see her
garnet hair, the green glint of beryl eyes.

She'll shimmer outside your bedroom
window, slip inside, dance electric
to a cosmic chorus, just for you.

Her throat-song seduces you with night
bird melodies—polyphony of whistles, chirps.

Her breath, a flute of wind, rushes over you,
overwhelms you like waves crashing the shore
in a storm; you are sand swirling back to sea.

Her siren's song is calling you back to her.
She's calling you home.

Spread your powdered wings, the Moon
isn't looking, and fly to her as a moth
of stardust; flutter to her hot hot light.

See Note [27]

Ceremony

After a reading by Joy Harjo

I look down from the wings of a great eagle,
a Muscogee song sifting through my feathers,
the wind singing prayers to my body below.

I sing to myself because I am a prayer even
after my spirit has gone—my body will stay
for a while for the ceremony we all need,

even as I was born, my mother washed me
with a flood of her love. Sponging her heart
into mine, I listened for her pulse as I drank in

her tenderness as soft as the whisper of milk.
Today, I am washed again with my memories
of her and of my children's—drenched in stars.

Pronounced *Mas ko' kee*

Transition

Prairie wind funnels dust
Into the heavenlies stirred up
By a white stallion. Chief's
Final gallop in this life.
Before the scarlet sun sets
Behind silhouetted sagebrush
Purpled by short hours, he prays
To the Great Spirit for safe
Transition to the otherworld.

His echo still rides haunting
The land. The long moon cries
But his sons have no war paint
on their faces. It was a good
Death.

Inspired by artwork in the Koshare Museum, La Junta, CO

References

[1] *Algonquian Legends*, Dover reprint (1992), Charles W. Leland 1884 book pubished by Houghton Mifflin. "This is the Song of the Stars" (Introduction to Section I); Abenaki Literature https://www.indigenouspeople.net/abnaki.htm; Four Poems in Passamaquoddy by Philip S. LeSourd (Indiana University), page 23-36 https://plesourd.com/wp-content/uploads/2019/03/Four-Poems-in-Passamaquoddy.pdf

[2] Winter Legends of the Northern Paiute: *How the Stars Got Their Twinkle and Why Coyote Howls to the Sky* https://osupress.oregonstate.edu/blog/winter-legends-of-northern-paiute

[3] Inspiration of the Spirit ("The Trees Wave Their Branches") http://www.inspirationforthespirit.com/native-american-wisdom/

[4] California Indian Education (Cree Prophecy following "After the Felling of Trees" and the Pueblo prayer in the Introduction to Section III) http://www.californiaindianeducation.org/inspire/traditional/

[5] Quotation from Chief Lawyer is cited from *The Western American Indian: Case Studies in Tribal History*, ed. Richard N. Ellis, "The Walla Walla Council of 1855" by Alvin M. Josephy, page 14, University of Nebraska Press, 1972. http://www.barnesandnoble.com/w/the-western-american-indian-richard-n-ellis/1112183285?ean=9780803257542

[6] Native American Proverbs (Postscript for "On a Quite Walkway," epigraph to "Pangaea," Introduction to Sections IV, V, & VII) http://ladysno.tripod.com/NativeAmerican.html

[7] Mohawk poem, "My Face" (Introduction to Section II) http://www.angelfire.com/md/elanmichaels/naquotations.html

[8] *A River Runs Through It*, Norman McClean, University of Chicago Press, 1989. The closing paragraph(s) serve as poem's epigraph.

[9] *American Indian Fairy Tales*, 2nd ed., Margaret Compton, Dodd, Meade & Company, New York, 1907. ("The Story Teller" is a redux and poetic adaptation of "The Story-teller Himself.")

[10] *Seneca Myths and Folk Tales*, Arthur C. Parker (Buffalo Historical Society, Publications Volume Twenty-seven) https://www.gutenberg.org/files/61477/61477-h/61477-h.htm; Plum-stone dice game https://www.museum.state.il.us/muslink/nat_amer/post/htmls/soc_plum.html

[11] *The Red Indian Fairy Book*, "The Story of the Star and Water Lilies," Frances Jenkins Olcott, Houghton Mifflin Company, Boston and New York, 1917 ("Little Wishing Star" is a poetic adaption of a Chippewa Story)

[12] *American Indian Myths and Legends*, Richard Erdoes and Alfonso Ortiz, Pantheon Books, New York, 1984, "The Legend of the Flute" (told by Henry Crow Dog to Richard Erdoes in 1967), pages 275–278 ("The Siyotanka" is a found poem from the text) and "The End of the World" (White River Sioux) inspired "Surviving Winter."

[13] Arawak Tribe of the Bahamas (The first tribe encountered by Christopher Columbus in the Americas), https://study.com/academy/lesson/arawak-tribe-history-language-symbols.html

[14] Access Genealogy, Blackfeet Religion ("The Lizard Wind") http://www.accessgenealogy.com/native/tribes/blackfeet/religion.htm

[15] Momaday's quote in the epigraph ("The Night the Stars Fell") found on New Perspectives on the West (http://www.shoppbs.pbs.org/weta/thewest/program/episodes/two/trailtears.htm). The source can be deduced from his own paraphrasing in Mountain Record: An American Land Ethic by N. Scott Momaday—a commentary on his book The Man Made of Words by N. Scott Momaday, St. Martin's Griffin, New York, "When the Stars Fell," page 170-171, July 15, 1998. (https://www.mountainrecord.org/earth-initiative/an-american-land-ethic/)

[16] The Ant People of the Hopi by Gary A. David ("Ant Hill People") https://www.ancient-origins.net/myths-legends-americas-opinion-guest-authors/ant-people-hopi-00927

[17] Butterfly Poems & Readings (Introduction to Section VI) http://www.folksbutterflyfarm.com/poem.htm

[18] Native American Butterfly Folklore (Footnote in "Whisperings") http://www.native-languages.org/legends-butterfly.htm

[19] Excerpt from *The Tale of the Wind Horse, a Native American Choctaw Legend* (Postscript in "Mending") https://warriornation.ning.com/group/stories-and-legends/forum/topics/the-tale-of-the-wind-horse

[20] Native American Wisdom (Epigraph for "On a Nature Trail") http://www.native-americans-online.com/native-american-wisdom-two.html

[21] Native American Proverbs and Wisdom (Postscript in "Morning Has Broken") https://www.legendsofamerica.com/na-proverbs/

[22] Young, John V. (1990). *Kokopelli: Casanova of the Cliff Dwellers; The hunchbacked flute player*. Filter Press. p. 18. ISBN 978-0-86541-026-8. ("Kokopelli")

[23] California Indian Education: Famous Indian Chiefs https://www.californiaindianeducation.org/famous_indian_chiefs/chief_seattle/ and *When Hubble Stared at Nothing for 100 Hours* by Nadia Drake ("Dark Matter") https://www.nationalgeographic.com/science/phenomena/2015/04/24/when-hubble-stared-at-nothing-for-100-hours/

[24] Native Heritage Project, *Tecumseh—"Die Like a Hero Going Home"* by Roberta Estes (Introduction to Section VII) https://nativeheritageproject.com/2013/11/17/tecumseh-die-like-a-hero-going-home/

[25] Popoluca might be a more general term but encompass the Mazahua and Purépecha tribes. The significance of the monarch butterfly is discussed below ("Monarch") https://listverse.com/2019/10/31/day-of-the-dead-facts/ and https://journeynorth.org/tm/monarch/SanctuaryFactsOyamel.html

[26] Grand County Colorado History, The Ute "Legend of the Canyons" (epigraph in "The Last Train") http://stories.grandcountyhistory.org/category/indian-legends

[27] The aurora boreales, the Northern Lights, are readily witnessed in northen latitudes, such as by the Inuit Indians in Alaska. ("Song of the Sun")

John C. Mannone has poems in *Anthology of Appalachian Writers XV* [Barbara Kingsver], *Red Branch Review*, *Windhover*, *North Dakota Quarterly*, *Adanna Literary Journal*, *Anacua Literary Arts Journal*, *Number One*, *Artemis Journal*, *Poetry South*, *Red Coyote*, *Blue Fifth Review*, *New England Journal of Medicine*, *Annals of Internal Medicine*, *Baltimore Review*, *Pedestal*, *Pirene's Fountain*, and others. He's a Jean Ritchie Fellowship winner in Appalachian literature (2017) and served as the celebrity judge for the National Federation of State Poetry Societies (2018). He has four poetry collections, and three chapbooks. He's been nominated for the Pushcart, Rhysling, and Best of the Net awards. He edits poetry for *Abyss & Apex* and *Silver Blade*. He's a professor of physics and nuclear safety consultant teaching mathematics in East Tennessee. He lives in Oak Ridge, TN. Visit the Art of Poetry/The Music of Words http://jcmannone.wordpress.com

www.ingramcontent.com/pod-product-compliance
Lightning Source LLC
Chambersburg PA
CBHW032123050726
47590CB00008B/2938